THE CIA IN XINJIANG
PART ONE

One Agent's Dubious Undertakings in Western China

Carter Ian Ames

ISBN-13: 978-1499679748
ISBN-10: 1499679742

To Peace

Chapter One
Introduction

"Fuck the State Department. You should apply to the CIA."

Those were the eloquent words of my college roommate when I told him that in addition to applying for some private companies, I was also going to submit an application to the State Department.

I decided to take the bait.

"Why do you think I should apply to the CIA?"

He retorted, "Well first of all, it'd be a hell ova lot more exciting than some mind numbed robot job at the State Department, and you'd accomplish greater things as well. Besides, with your language aptitude, you'd be a perfect fit."

I remained unconvinced, but on a lark, after I submitted my application to State, I also spent the time and submitted one to the CIA.

This was in the fall of 2005. In May of the following year I would graduate from Berkeley with a degree in Linguistics, along with minors in Chinese and political science.

I had an interest in languages from an early age. My father was a pilot for United Airlines, and the biggest perk of that job was we were able to fly for free. Our parents saw the value in exposing us to different cultures and languages, and they also liked to see new places.

Even as kids, we went on trips to foreign countries. Often, months before those trips our father would come home with foreign language CDs for me and my sister to try and learn a bit of the language of the country we would visit.

By the time I was eighteen I had been to most of Europe, part of Asia and to Australia.

My interest in Chinese was not as a result of a visit. I had actually never been there. As a kid, I was infatuated with Bruce Lee and his movies and even became somewhat proficient in martial arts. By the time I entered college, I had this crazy dream of spending a year in Beijing studying kung fu. In addition to studying kung fu, I had been listening to Chinese language CDs for years, even before college.

Now I was nearing graduation and it was time to be realistic. I had applied to graduate school to study international relations, but quite honestly, I was rather sick of school and would rather work.

I figured with the right job, I may be able to live overseas, or at least do significant international travel.

The application process for the government jobs could take from a matter of a few months up to a year.

For the State Department position, I had to register for and take the Foreign Service Officer Test (FSOT) which was given three times a year.

By March of 2006, I was invited to take the test for the State Department. I went to San Francisco to take it. The test had three multiple-choice sections. The first section was job knowledge which included questions about the U.S. government, U.S. and world history, psychology, finance and some other areas.

I felt good about everything except psychology. I took one psych class in college and got a C. The only concept I remembered was that the only difference between the shrink and the patient was who had the keys to the office.

The other two sections were English language proficiency, and personality type questions.

About half way through the test the administrators caught one guy near me pulling out a piece of paper presumably trying to cheat. It reminded me of Chevy Chase in the movie "Spies Like Us."

It seemed all the more ridiculous in that unless he had someone on the inside who gave him a list of correct answers, I wasn't sure how a cheat sheet was going to be much help with this type of test.

He was escorted out, and shortly after that I finished the test and left. I was fairly optimistic that I did sufficiently well and thought I would be asked to continue with the application process.

In the last week of March, I had an interview with an insurance company for a claims position. Half way through the interview, I knew this was purely a backup that I hoped I would not need.

In the beginning of April, I was contacted by the CIA, and invited for an interview in San Francisco the following week.

I was told not to tell anyone except immediate family members that I was seeking employment with the CIA.

When my roommate asked me where I was going, I told him I had an interview with someone from the State Department.

The next day, I was contacted by a heavy machinery corporation that I had applied to. They produced most of their products in China and were looking for a manager who would be based out of China. They asked me to come in for an interview the following day.

I was interviewed by two managers, Jon and Mike. Jon was a stuffed shirt and Mike was a bit looser. Mike asked me about my willingness to relocate to China. This was wonderful news, and of course I told them I was interested. They had plants in a couple different places in China, but told me I could likely pick which city I wanted to live in.

Half way through the interview, Mike answered a call (on speaker phone) from a Chinese manager in China. He put the call on speaker. They told the manager they were interviewing me. He introduced himself as Joe (obviously he used an English name with us, and this was not his given name).

Joe started talking to me in Chinese, and we had a few minute conversation. It was obviously planned between them ahead of time to test my Chinese language ability, which was fine.

At the end of our conversation in Chinese, Mike picked up the phone and he and Joe spoke for a minute. Mike then hung up and told me that Joe liked my Chinese. I told Mike it needed work. I spoke with the partners a bit more and then they said they would be in touch with me.

This potential job was now at the top of my list. I could live overseas, in Beijing no less, and the application process for the government jobs could take many more months. Even if I was offered a government job, there was no guarantee where it would be.

A couple days later a manager from the insurance company called and offered me the job. I told her I would consider it and get back to her.

The next week I went for the interview with the CIA. It was in a non-descript office in the federal building in San Francisco.

I thought maybe I would be interviewed by several people, but it was one guy named Bob Jones, which I figured was not his real name.

He asked me why I applied for a position as an operations officer as opposed to some other position.

I told him I didn't want to be chained to a desk all day in Virginia, and would like to live abroad, and utilize my interest in other languages and cultures.

He then asked me if I was fluent in Chinese. I told him I could communicate verbally, but my reading and writing needed some work.

We also talked about my international travel as a kid and what other languages I was exposed to.

He then said, "I see you also applied to the State Department. Anywhere else?"

I told him I applied to some corporations and had an interview at a machinery firm with production facilities in China, and was offered a job handling insurance claims.

I figured he was interested in me when he started talking me out of the other positions.

He said, "Well, if you don't want to be chained to a desk, I'm not sure the State Department is right for you because you will spend most of your time in an office. That's nothing compared this machinery corporation. Yes you will get to live overseas, but they will have you working until midnight, if you're lucky. You'll never see or experience much of China with that job because even when you travel, you will be working most of the time. As far as insurance, you'll be bored with that in a week. It sounds like the CIA is the best fit for your interests."

He then asked, "Would China be your first preference for overseas assignment?"

I answered, "Yes, but I'm open to other countries as well."

The truth is I really wanted to go to China, but did not want to seem rigid, and I truly would have gone elsewhere if this was the best job on the table.

He asked me if I had any questions.

I asked, "How long does this process normally take?"

He said, "It can take up to a year, but we are trying to get that down to a couple to three months."

He then told me the next step in the process was the polygraph.

He said, "During the polygraph, the examiner will probably ask you extensive details about your drug use. I noticed on your application you've smoked a fair amount of marijuana."

I said, "That was a requirement for my field of study at Berkeley."

He laughed and said, "In the past, that would have been a problem, but the agency has taken a different view about drug use, especially if it's only marijuana."

He paused a bit as if he was waiting for me to answer, even though it wasn't a question.

I said, "Yes, only marijuana. I never tried the hard stuff."

He said, "Well, again, that shouldn't be a problem. Just know those questions are coming during the polygraph and be honest."

Around the middle of May, on a Wednesday, I received an email from the State Department advising me that I achieved a satisfactory score on the FSOT and that I needed to complete a Personal Narrative (PN).

The PN was an essay I was to write that would provide examples of my skills and abilities in terms of leadership, interpersonal and communication skills among other things. I was given three weeks to complete this task.

The next day Mike from the machinery firm called and arranged a second interview over lunch.

On Friday, I met Mike and Jon at their office.

Mike asked, "How does Chinese food sound?"

I said, "That would be great."

We went to an upscale Chinese restaurant. They asked me to do the ordering, in Chinese. I didn't tell them that Chinese in San Francisco were more likely to speak Cantonese than Mandarin, but I figured most could also understand Mandarin.

The waitress came and I ordered. She understood, and asked me how I knew how to speak Chinese.

The guys asked me where I would want to live in China, if I thought I would have a problem with culture shock from living in another country as opposed to just visiting one, what my salary expectations were, and many other questions.

They asked what questions I had. I asked them about visa procedures, their time frame for making a decision, some specifics about the scope of the job and some other questions.

It was a good lunch and meeting, and they told me they would be in touch in the near future.

I spent almost all of that weekend working on and editing my PN for the State Department. By Monday morning I was happy with it and sent it to them.

On Wednesday, I received a call from Bob from the CIA to arrange my polygraph. He asked if Friday would be alright. I agreed and he told me to meet him at the federal building at 8 am.

On Thursday, Mike called and offered me the position with the machinery company. He told me I did not have to accept the offer that day and that a written offer was on its way to me. I thanked him and told him I would be in touch.

That afternoon, I called the manager at the insurance company and thanked her, but informed her I was going in a different direction. Even if nothing panned out with the government jobs, a job located in China was preferable to insurance claims in the bay area.

Friday came and I met Bob at the federal building. When I walked into the office he was chatting with another guy. Bob introduced him as Larry, and told me he had worked in China before.

Larry started talking to me in Chinese. This was obviously the CIAs test of my Chinese language ability. I was starting to get used to this.

We talked for about five minutes, and then Larry looked at Bob and said, "Well, he can speak Chinese."

Bob chuckled and then walked me into a back room where the polygraph examiner was sitting. He introduced me to the examiner, but did not give me his name.

The exam took hours, and as Bob told me, in addition to questions about practically everything, he asked a lot of questions about drug use. He wanted make sure I had not used other drugs besides marijuana, or maybe just wanted to see if I was being honest.

When I finished Bob had me sit in the front office for a minute while he talked to the examiner. Bob then took me to a sandwich shop for lunch. He asked me how my other job prospects were going.

I told him I got the job with the machinery company in China, the insurance company and that the State Department job process was continuing.

He told me the State Department job could take many more months to pan out. He then asked me not to take the job with the machinery or insurance company.

He surprised me by saying, "We want you. Now that we know you can communicate in Chinese, and you passed your polygraph, we should be able to conclude your background check soon and offer you a position."

I told him that sounded great and I looked forward to hearing from him.

I went home and spent the weekend thinking about the CIA job versus the machinery company.

Bob was probably right about the long hours I would spend at the machinery company. Still, it appeared they would let me live in Beijing, and surely there would be some time to do stuff I wanted to do. Also, it was guaranteed that with them, I would live in China. With the CIA, I could end up just about anywhere on earth.

However, I must admit the excitement of being a spy was too powerful to resist. Also, maybe I wouldn't like China as much as I thought

I would. With the CIA, likely I would have opportunities to work in multiple countries whereas the machinery company was clearly a one country situation. If offered the position with the CIA, I was going to take it.

One week later Mike from the machinery company called. He asked me if I considered their offer.

I told him I had and was deciding between theirs and one other. Of course I had not heard back from Bob, but figured either I would hear from him soon like he said or if not, I would accept Mike's offer. I told Mike I would give them an answer within a week.

A few days later Bob called and offered me the job at the CIA.

I accepted it on the spot. He told me someone would be in touch with me in the near future to organize my travel to Virginia. He also told me not to tell any other potential future employers where I was going to work.

I called Mike and thanked him for the offer, but told him I accepted another offer.

He asked where I was going to work. I told him I was going to work for the State Department. He sounded a bit surprised, but thanked me for considering his company.

The next day I received a call from a Washington DC phone number. I figured it was the person Bob referenced. Instead, it was someone from the State Department inviting me to take the Oral Assessment (OR).

I thanked her, but advised her I had accepted another position elsewhere. After I hung up, I wondered for a minute how different that job might have been, if I had gotten it, but then decided it was best to put the what ifs out of my mind.

Chapter Two
The Journey Begins

A few days later I received a call from a woman who gave me flight information. I would be flying to Washington in a week.

She gave me an address and told me to take a taxi there. There would be a key under the mat, and the next day another CT (career trainee) would join me. She also told me to bring my ids including driver's license and passport with me.

I arrived in DC in the middle of June of 2006. I took a taxi as instructed. The key was where she said it would be.

On the ride in, I noticed some restaurants within walking distance. I went to a Chinese restaurant that night.

The next morning, my roommate showed up. We said hello, and he did not offer his name, so neither did I.

A few hours later, a couple people from Langley arrived including the woman I spoke with on the phone.

She asked for both of our ids. I gave her my driver's license. She asked me where my passport was, and I told her when I tried to dig it up back home, I could not find it.

That was a lie. I don't know what it was, but the idea of being without any form of legal id was more than I could deal with this early in the process. Besides, what if after a few days at the farm I cracked under the pressure, and wanted to get on the first flight back home. I could just picture them telling me, "Sorry, we lost your id."

She handed us both a military id. It said I was in the army reserves. My name on it was Carter Ian Ames.

They took us to the farm which is just outside of Williamsburg, Virginia. It took about two and a half hours for the actual drive. We stopped half way and had lunch.

They spent part of the time in the car giving us a bit of a preview of the training from surveillance detection training, paramilitary training and tradecraft.

We arrived at the farm and they showed each of us to our separate rooms.

As I was unpacking, one of the instructors walked in and introduced himself as Joe. He was a portly, balding guy in his 50s with a warn face.

I started to introduce myself and was not sure which name to use. Then I figured if they gave me a cover name, they expected me to use it.

Just as I was about to say Carter, he said, "Use the name we give you, with everyone here and elsewhere, unless and until we give you another identity."

He then said, "I wanted to talk to you a little bit about your background and where we might place you."

I said, "Ok."

He then asked, "When you think of the normal duties of a case officer, what do you imagine you would typically be doing?"

I felt like this was another stage of the interview process that I was already done with, but I played along.

I answered, "Identifying foreigners who have information of interest to the U.S. government, identifying their potential weaknesses or vulnerabilities, and then exploiting those weaknesses and paying them money to get them to turn over information to us."

He said, "That is textbook. That is exactly what we normally do. In your case, we have a bit of a different assignment in mind."

He continued, "Normally, we wait a few months and see how your training is going before we talk about potential assignments, but the posting we have in mind for you is unique, and we think it is best that you start with the language study right away. How familiar are you with western China?"

"Not very," I replied.

He then threw me for a loop when he said, "We would like you to go to Xinjiang."

Xinjiang, I thought to myself. I had heard of the place, but was not at all familiar with it. Besides, I was really hoping for Beijing.

Like a mind reader, he then said, "I know, you were probably hoping for Shanghai or Beijing."

I chuckled a bit and replied, "Beijing would be nice."

He said, "We've got case officers coming out of our ears in Beijing both out of the embassy and not official cover, but we don't have much on the ground intelligence in western China, and with your background you will be a good fit for the cover we have in mind."

He continued, "In regards to your assignment, we don't see you recruiting spies, at least not in the beginning. The Chinese are suspicious of foreigners, and most are so patriotic to the point of nationalistic that it is a delicate and dangerous game to try to randomly recruit a local there that you have not known for some time. It's dangerous to recruit there even if you do know them a long time. Accordingly, we don't want you to try and recruit people when you first get there. Besides, we have other activities in mind for you."

"What's that?" I asked.

He replied, "That's not important right now, but let's talk about your cover."

I asked, "What did you have in mind for that?"

He responded, "We're going to make you an English teacher. You have a degree in linguistics, so it's a perfect fit. The only thing is, in addition preparing you for that a bit, we want you to start studying the Uyghur language immediately. Here. Take a look at this tonight."

He gave me a binder full of papers and a computer.

He then said, "That is some background information on Xinjiang and a computer with Uyghur language lessons already installed on it. Read the background information tonight and try to do at least one hour of language study per night while you are here. Also, don't tell any of the other CTs or anyone else about this. Study Uyghur at night, when you are by yourself in your room so no one else will know."

Just as I was about to leave he said," Oh, also, in terms of your training here, pay particularly close attention to the surveillance detection and paramilitary training. It will be very important where you are going."

Excuse me? I walked out of his office and nearly dropped a load in my pants. They don't want me to recruit spies and I have to be good at surveillance detection and paramilitary operations. This is not good.

I immediately began thinking this is not what I had in mind. I was going to go to Beijing, study martial arts, eat Kung Pao Chicken and hit the tourist spots, but instead they want me to go to Xinjiang and be good at detecting surveillance and paramilitary operations. Xinjiang? What's in Xinjiang? Surveillance detection? Ok, all case officers have to be good at that, but paramilitary operations? You don't even have to successfully complete that at the farm, and you can still become a case officer, so why did I need to be good at it? I couldn't believe this.

Why did I listen to my roommate? I should be at the State Department oral exam right now or managing a tractor factory from my home in Beijing. Oh my

God, what have I done? I suppose I could grab my passport and run.

Then cooler heads prevailed. I told myself, that I knew all along that I could be sent anywhere in the world. At least I got the country I wanted, maybe I would like it in the west, and I might get a chance to move to Beijing later.

After I calmed down back in my room, I pulled out the background info he gave me about Xinjiang and started reading it.

According to the information he gave me, I learned that Xinjiang is China's most northwest province, directly north of Tibet. It has the largest population of Uyghur people (commonly pronounced wegur) anywhere in the world. They are concentrated in the southern part of the province.

They are a Turkic people, and speak Uyghur language, which is a Turkic language, although the official language in Xinjiang (like the rest of China) is Mandarin.

Most Uyghurs are Muslims while most Han (the majority Chinese ethnicity) do not practice any religion.

Many of the Uyghurs regard the region as East Turkistan. The Uyghurs argue that they have lived independently for millenniums, and the Han dispute this.

China has exercised control over the territory since 1949, and the Chinese government would argue much longer than that.

Historically, most of the population was Uyghur, although since 1949, the Chinese government has had a policy of encouraging Han to move to Xinjiang. This has resulted in the population of Han in Xinjiang going from six percent decades ago to forty percent today.

Uyghurs complain that Han get the best jobs in Xinjiang, and that restrictions on them like requiring their beards to be shaved and women not wearing headscarves is diluting their culture.

Some Uyghurs want full independence and some simply want more autonomy and their traditions respected by the government.

Beijing is likely to grant none of this, especially independence or autonomy. Xinjiang is home to vast oil and gas reserves, not to mention rare earth minerals.

Not only is Xinjiang home to this largess, but it is also the location in China where pipelines from Central Asian nations deliver resources to China.

This year (2006), a crude oil pipeline
designed to deliver 200,000 barrels per day of crude oil from Kazakhstan to China
became operational. More are planned.

The potential of the region to deliver energy resources to China in a cost-efficient manner are nearly limitless, assuming other factors.

For instance, China has long term contracts with Iran to buy its oil for decades to come.

Currently, that oil gets to China by tankers on the sea. However, if there were to be a stable Afghanistan or Pakistan and a stable Xinjiang, there is no reason a pipeline could not be built saving China tremendous amounts of money in the long run and ensuring reliable delivery of oil. This would be a huge benefit to the Chinese economy.

I really didn't like where all this was going, and was surprised the briefing material I was given was so candid.

Part of me thought maybe they were being up front with me, so I could decide now if this was for me, so we would not waste each other's time. Was a lateral to the State Department out of the question? I realized even asking that question out loud, as a joke, would be a career killer for me.

He also gave me a small amount of information about Bangkok, Thailand. It was almost like the information a travel agent would give a tourist who was going there for the first time. I had no idea why he gave it to me, but I read it as well.

The next morning Joe came in my room and asked if I had read the material he gave me. I told him I had.

He asked, "What do you think?"

I answered, "It sounds like a complicated place with a lot of interested parties."

He chuckled and said, "That's a very careful answer, but also very true."

We can talk about it more at a later time.

For now, in terms of what I told you yesterday about your cover, we have to start laying the groundwork. Our first option is to try to get you into Xinjiang Normal University in Urumqi under the

English Fellows Program. The requirements for it are a master's in linguistics or TESOL, and two years' overseas teaching experience."

"I only have a bachelor's, and no teaching experience" I said.

He replied, "I know that. Don't worry about that. We've already built a resume for you with your bachelor's in linguistics like you have, but also a master's in TESOL as well as two years teaching experience in Bangkok. This will all be under your cover name, and it will all be verifiable. We will give you a resume, transcripts and references all under your cover name, and they will all check out. When the time is right, we'll have you apply for that job. That job is funded by the State Department, so we'll make some calls and should be able to put you in that position."

At that moment I was thinking how fast this was all moving, and I hadn't even had my training yet.

I asked him, "Who do you know in Bangkok?"

He answered, "A semi-retired agent who during his time in Bangkok in addition to picking up a case of gonorrhea, picked up a Thai wife. She didn't want to leave Thailand. He lives in Bangkok with her, and runs a small English school which is a front for us for various purposes. It's a perfect fit for your cover."

He continued, "Now, in case you don't get the English fellows position, we're also going to have you take a trip over to Xinjiang in the near future and visit some other colleges. Our information indicates that teachers who make a trip to universities in China ahead of time and apply in person, have a much better chance of getting a job."

I asked, "Will that trip be during a break in the training here?"

He replied, "Yes, or we can fit you into another group of CTs for whatever you miss. That is not a big deal."

He went on, "Lastly, we need to give you a job for this year for a couple reasons. We want to fill in your resume for this year while you are at the farm so it doesn't look like you were just sitting on your mom's couch for twelve months, but also the State Department has advised us that the Chinese government, maybe in an attempt to keep out rabble rousers during the Olympics, might start requiring new English teachers to have two or three years of work experience before they can get a visa to teach English. We will build a cover for you as an editor's assistant for a big publishing house. That's plausible considering your degree, and that way if they start requiring three years of work experience, you will have that by next autumn. We are going to start paying you by direct deposit from that job. I need you to go to the bank today with someone from the farm that I will introduce you to and open an account."

I said, "You took my id and I only have a military id with my new name."

He said, "I almost forgot. Here is your new passport with your new name. Take this with your military id, and that will be enough to open a bank account. We've already opened a P.O. Box for you. Use that as your mailing address and we'll give you an address to use for your physical address. Now, let me go get Michelle to go with you."

He left and I sat in my room. I looked in the passport which showed its issue date as a couple years ago. It had work visas, residence permits and exit and entry stamps for Thailand. I was there about five minutes until a woman walked in. I introduced myself.

She said, "Hello, I'm Michelle. I'm going to take you to the bank. You'll need a new social security number and date of birth to correspond with your new identity. Here they are along with the physical address you'll give to the bank. Memorize them before we get to the bank, and then destroy this piece of paper."

She asked me to bring my passport and military id.

On the way to the car she said, "If anyone asks you about your military service, your cover is you are infantry in the army reserves."

We got in the car and then she laid it all out for me.

She said, "The bank will ask you your occupation. Tell them you are an editor's assistant at Wikes and Eckelman publishers. Open a savings and a checking account with a debit card. We'll use the checking to directly deposit your paycheck from the publisher. The money in this account is only to be spent by you for official business such as buying a plane ticket to China, and expenses while there. When you do go to China for one week or one year, only bring this bank ATM/debit card with you. Don't bring any bank information from the account we set up to pay you your CIA paycheck. Also, never check that account online from China."

We arrived at the bank, and she gave me three thousand dollars cash to put in the new account.

I went inside and asked to open up a new account. I put fifteen hundred in the savings and fifteen in the checking.

The woman asked where I worked, and asked me for two forms of ID. I gave her the passport and military id.

She said, "I thought you worked for a publisher?"

I responded, "I do. I am not active duty military. I'm in the reserves."

She said, "Oh, I see."

Fifteen minutes later I was finished and went back to Michelle's car.

We went back to the farm where I spent the next weeks learning/practicing surveillance detection.

At its most basic level, this involved activities such as driving in town and on the freeway and seeing if anyone was following me, and if so, reporting their description as well as their vehicle description to my superiors.

About two weeks into it Michelle came to my room and told me we needed to run an errand.

We went to the house whose address I used when I opened my bank account. On the way, we stopped at the post office and got my mail. My mail consisted of my ATM/debit card from the bank along with some other correspondence from the bank about online banking and other matters. I also received a Virginia driver's license under the name Carter Ian Ames.

I said to Michelle, "I didn't know I applied for a driver's license."

She smiled and said, "You did."

We arrived at the house, and sat at a desk with a computer at it. She had me set up an email address using my cover name. Next I set up online banking, and was able to view my accounts. I saw that a paycheck from my cover job was already directly deposited into my checking account.

She then had me apply for a four week course on teaching English to foreigners. This was news to me.

She said, "You won't need this to get a job in China, especially with the resume we built for you, but since you don't have teaching experience, we think this will be beneficial for you."

She pulled out a resume with a school listed in New Mexico for my two degrees.

She said, "This is a good choice because chances are no other teacher you run into will have gone to this same university. Most of the Americans teaching in China are from the west coast or east coast."

I asked, "If a school in China contacts this university in New Mexico, will they verify my degrees?"

She looked at me with total confusion and said, "Of course."

I felt like I was spending more time on building a cover as a teacher, than on becoming a spy.

The next day the school that I was to take the four week class at emailed me a pre-interview task designed to test my knowledge of grammar, and with some hypothetical classroom situations and asking me how I would handle them.

I completed it and emailed it back to them.

The next day a manager from the school called and interviewed me for about twenty minutes.

She asked me some questions related to the task I completed, and some questions like how I would teach the meaning of particular words to students.

At the end of the interview, she accepted me into their class starting in November.

In October I finished surveillance detection training (although as long as you are at the farm you are never really finished with it), and thankfully I passed. One CT did not. The word was that he failed to detect two different cars following him on a particular exercise. As a result, he was offered a desk job at Langley or the front door. He accepted the desk job.

At the end of October, Joe came into my room and told me to make hotel reservations for the class I was going to take on teaching English to foreigners. He told me to use the bank account I set up with Michelle to pay for all food and lodging for the class.

The class was in Washington DC which was too far from the farm to commute each day. I booked a hotel close to the school's location, and it was not cheap.

The following week the class started, and it was intense. We were in class all day, and spent much of the evenings preparing lessons.

The students we were teaching were immigrants of all different ethnicities. Some were Chinese. I found out one was from Xinjiang.

The class was beneficial, but after four weeks I was definitely happy to be done.

If I thought the class was tough, when it finished I started paramilitary training which put things into perspective.

Everyone in the group I trained with had prior military experience, except me. Many of them had some type of special forces experience.

We practiced shooting various firearms, self-defense tactics, how to kill without weapons, how to make and use rudimentary weapons, repelling from mountains with ropes, reading topographic and other types of maps, making improvised explosive devices, and detonating various explosives.

At one point we were sent to a rural location, given a map, and had to travel for twenty-four hours straight through various terrains to get to a location.

All of the above I could handle. What had me a little spooked was when they asked us to jump out of an airplane.

I definitely had to psych myself up for that one. I kept telling myself it would be over before I knew it, and it was.

My fright was building all the way until I actually jumped, and then my emotions turned to concentration to pull the cord at the right time, and when I was on the ground, it was a feeling of exhilaration.

The paramilitary training was particularly grueling, but also helped me to get in great shape. It also boosted my confidence to face any challenge, physical or otherwise.

In early January Michelle took me back to my residence of record and we sat at the same desk.

From the same computer she had me fill out the online application for the teaching fellows program. She produced transcripts for me to submit.

She also had me buy a plane ticket to China to leave in a couple weeks. She had me buy one ticket to Beijing and back, and a separate ticket to Xinjiang, so it would look like I was doing the touristy thing in Beijing for a few days before going to Xinjiang to look for work. I also booked hotels in both cities.

I then downloaded the visa application form for China. It asked the names of family members. I hadn't thought about that yet. Michelle gave me the names of my parents and one brother.

Michelle then had me go on a website with a list of teaching jobs in China and had me contact several universities in Xinjiang and send them emails asking for an interview when I would be there.

The visa application form also asked my itinerary in China. Michelle had me list the days in Beijing and names of a couple of the schools in Xinjiang that I contacted.

Michelle also had me call the bank and notify them I would be taking a trip to China and might use my ATM card there.

The next morning, I went to the Chinese embassy in DC.

On my way there, I noticed a white Altima near the beginning of my trip, and an hour later on the freeway.

I had hoped I was done with surveillance detection tests, but we were told in the beginning that we might be tested at any point during our training. I wrote down the vehicle and license plate information as well as description of the driver to turn in when I got back to the farm.

I arrived at the embassy and submitted my passport, the visa application and fee. They said it would be ready in four days.

Four days later, I went back to the embassy and picked up my passport with the visa inside it.

I received responses from two universities asking me to contact them when I arrived in Xinjiang and set up a time for an interview.

In preparation for my trip, Michelle and Joe sat me down and told me a few things.

The first thing they told me was not to lose my passport.

I looked at them and said, "You realize, I've done this before, without ever losing a passport."

Joe responded, "Yet when we asked you to bring your passport to us when we picked you up, you told us you couldn't find it."

I had forgotten about that (maybe because I didn't really lose it) and said, "Point taken."

He went on, "We're only telling you this because we don't want you to have to visit the embassy while you are in China."

They also told me to hit up some tourist spots in Beijing like the Forbidden City and Summer Palace to play the part of a tourist.

Joe then told me to spend some time in Urumqi out and about and try to become familiar with the layout of the city.

They also reminded me not to check my personal bank account or any type of internet based accounts associated with my real name online from China.

They gave me some money in Chinese currency, but told me to try to withdraw money using my ATM card once I arrived in Beijing and in Xinjiang to confirm it would work in China.

Joe asked me, "If the schools ask you why you want to live and teach in Xinjiang, what will you tell them."

I thought for a minute and said, "I'll tell them I want to experience a place a little off the beaten path to experience the real China."

He said, "That will work."

Joe told me not to use any Uyghur language that I had learned so far. He told me that it would not be unusual nowadays for a westerner to speak decent Mandarin, but a western who had never lived in Xinjiang who spoke good Uyghur might set off alarm bells.

Then Joe told me I was going to meet Mike Stevens in Beijing. He worked out of the consulate in Chengdu, Sichuan Province and he would be my boss once I moved to China. Joe showed me a picture of him, but advised me he might look different when I met him.

Joe advised me to go to the Summer Palace two days after my arrival in Beijing, at 10 am and Mike would find me.

Finally, Michelle mentioned the obvious. If I did run into some kind of trouble I could contact the embassy, but under no circumstances should I call Langley while in China.

Chapter Three
China and Back

The following week I took a car to the DC airport. In late January 2007, there was not yet a nonstop flight from DC to Beijing, so I caught a flight to Detroit, and from there, got a flight direct to Beijing.

I arrived just before 3 pm the following day (Tuesday) in Beijing. As we were descending, there was one point where the air went from bright blue to a brown haze. This was China's nasty air pollution I had heard about.

Upon arrival, I walked quite a distance to immigration. After a short wait there, I walked past customs and into the arrival hall. I had a small bag on wheels and one backpack.

I found an ATM and was able to get cash with it.

Then I went outside and got in the line for cabs. I think I had to wait longer for a cab than in line at immigration.

After about twenty minutes I got in a cab and told him the name of the hotel in Chinese.

The driver commented on my pronunciation and asked me (in Chinese) how I knew Chinese.

I told him I studied for many years in America. He talked the entire way to the hotel.

I picked a reasonably priced hotel close to the Forbidden City and Wanfujing which was a famous shopping street.

I checking into the hotel and did a little unpacking. It was now about five pm. I walked around Wangfujing and at some points I felt like I was back home. There was everything from McDonalds to Haagen-Dazs. There were also many Chinese brands.

I found a bunch of outdoor food stalls on a side street called the Donghuamen Night Market. They had everything from dumplings to deep fried scorpions.

I had some dumplings and did a little people watching while I ate.

I walked back towards the hotel and came across a small convenience store. I went in and bought some bottled water and snacks.

Later, I went to Houhai which is a small lake with bars all around it. It was packed with people, both Chinese and foreigners.

I only had a couple drinks before I hit a wall and took a taxi back to the hotel.

While I was out and about, without even thinking about it I found myself trying to detect surveillance. While on foot I think I did an ok job, but as a passenger in the back seat of a taxi, it was a bit difficult. I did not detect any surveillance.

The next day I went to the Forbidden City and a good Chinese restaurant.

On Thursday, I went to the Summer Palace as instructed at 10 am. I bought a ticket and walked around.

After about ten minutes Mike approached me.

He said, "Good morning Ian."

I said, "Good morning Mike."

"How are you my friend?" he asked.

"A little jet lagged, but happy to be in China," I answered.

He looked different than the picture Joe showed me. He looked to be in his mid to late 50s. He was wearing a hat and big sunglasses. In person, his hair had color but was gray in the picture I was shown. He also had a big belly, but not so in the picture. I think part of his getup was a disguise.

We walked as we talked.

He asked me, "Have you read the briefing materials that Joe gave you?'

I replied, "Yes."

He then asked, "What do you see as the strategic interest we have in Xinjiang."

I said, "Resources."

He said, "That's a big part of it. There are huge oil and gas resources in Xinjiang with more being discovered regularly. It's also an actual or potential place for China to get resources delivered from other countries like Iran and

Kazakhstan. We can't access any of those resources ourselves now, but we can do the next best thing which is making it difficult and costly for China to access them. Ok, what else related to resources?"

"I'm not sure where you're headed," I said.

He said, "In the briefing materials you were given, it talked about some segment of the Uyghurs want not just autonomy, but an independent state, right?"

"Yeah, I read that," I said.

He continued, "Well, some of us have not given up on that as a possibility. Imagine if that ever happens. Not only will we have access to all those resources, but we would be able to put U.S. military bases there, one step closer to encircling Beijing. Imagine what it does to their dreams regarding Taiwan if they have to worry about a U.S. airbase in their backyard? Ok, but that is not going to happen in the near future, so what else besides resources?"

"The more China is bogged down in western China with groups wanting independence/autonomy, the less attention it can pay to Taiwan," I said.

"Absolutely he said, but not just Taiwan. China has grand plans for the East and South China Seas which are full of resources, and is making claims over Islands that belong to other countries. They are massively increasing their military budget, especially their navy, so anything we can do to divert their attention out west is a good thing."

I asked, "How advanced is their military?"

He said, "A lot more advanced than it should be. They beg, borrow or steal everything, especially military technology. Do you remember when one of our F-117A Stealth Fighters was shot down over Yugoslavia?"

"Vaguely," I answered.

He continued, "Well, Chinese personnel from the embassy in Belgrade fanned out across the area with wads of cash and paid farmers for pieces of the plane. They brought them to Beijing, and were able to reverse engineer the material, and now they have stealth planes."

I said, "But I would guess they can't go head to head with us militarily."

He replied, "That's true, but they're not planning to. As an example, this hasn't been made public yet, but a few weeks ago they shot down one of their own satellites from space."

I asked, "Why did they do that?"

He said, "It was an old satellite they did not need anymore, and they wanted to see if they could do it. They also wanted to send a big fuck you to the good old US of A. Imagine if we get in a shooting war with them over Taiwan, and they shoot down our military satellites. Suddenly our ships, planes and missiles have no navigation and are practically useless and defenseless. Additionally, they have some very sophisticated missiles that could take out an aircraft carrier or destroyer. As a result, we need to keep what I would call a soft war, from becoming a shooting war."

I said, "A soft war? Are you saying we are already at war with them?"

He said, "Absolutely. Again, not a shooting war, but a low intensity asymmetrical war, absolutely. This is not a State Department position you are taking on. And it's only going to get dicier as they become stronger and stronger militarily and think they are the new captain of the pacific."

He then said, "But you have this unique opportunity to do a great service for your country. Our efforts could actually prevent a war with China. To that end we need constant tension out in the west, so the Uyghurs are our friends.

They don't like Beijing, and we don't like Beijing."

I said, "I also suppose they can do things we can't."

He said, "That's the kind of thinking I like to hear. There are certain things we can't have an American caught doing out in the west, but if a Uyghur gets caught doing, China can't successfully blame us for it. For instance, when you here about violence and what the Chinese government calls terrorist attacks in Xinjiang, you always hear the words rudimentary weapons. We trained Uyghurs in how to successfully use such weapons. They can do significant damage with them, and we have deniability. Then when China blames outside forces for such attacks, they look paranoid. It's a thing of beauty."

He then delved into logistics.

He said, "Obviously when you are living in Xinjiang, we can't pick up the phone and call each other. We're not the only country that monitors all calls and email. One benefit to being a teacher is you will have a lot of breaks. We'll meet during those. You'll come to Chengdu once or twice as a tourist, you'll go to Beijing and other cities and maybe I will meet you there. Possibly someone else will meet you. I may also come to Xinjiang once and meet up with you. And during your long summer break you'll go back to Langley. How's your Uyghur language studying coming along?

I said, "I study every day. I think I am becoming conversational."

He said, "Good. Keep that up, but when you first arrive in Xinjiang during this trip and when you first start teaching, don't let on to any Han that you are fluent or conversational in Uyghur. Now when you deal with Uyghurs, a few can speak Mandarin and some can speak English, so you may not always have to speak to them in Uyghur, but with some you will have to so keep studying."

He then said, "After you've settled in a while, we see you acting in not only a liaison role but also a paramilitary role as opposed to intelligence. Besides, our best source of intelligence in the west right now is signals intelligence."

"Paramilitary? I thought we agreed there are things an American cannot get caught doing?" I asked.

"That's right," he said, "So you are not going to get caught. And that my friend is lesson number one. Never, ever get caught. When you get back to the farm, not while you are in China, the first thing I want you to do is look up Amnesty's report from 1999 on torture in Xinjiang. The short version is one of their techniques is inserting horse hairs or wires with barbs into the penis of Uyghur prisoners."

"Oh no," I said.

"Oh yes," he responded. "Abu Ghraib has nothing on the Chinks. They invented torture."

I was more than a little turned off by his racist term for the Chinese. Then again, I figured it made it easier to justify any tactic against the Chinese if you dehumanized them in your own mind.

I then said, "You mentioned signals intelligence. I would have thought that would be a little soft in Western China."

He laughed and said, "It was at one time, but I'll let you in on a little secret. We have a listening post on the roof of the Chengdu consulate masquerading as an air conditioning unit. That's not all we have at the consulate, but I can't go into that. We have another listening post at a military outpost in eastern Afghanistan which is one of the many reasons we can't and won't completely pull all our troops out of Afghanistan. If we leave Afghanistan, so will our listening post, not to mention the Afghans will be more likely to sign deals with the Chinese to sell their resources. You know

Afghanistan has a lot more natural resources than most people realize. Rumor has it we also have a listening post in Mongolia, but I have not been able to confirm that."

I asked him, "Is there anything in particular I should bring with me when I come back to teach?"

He said, "Yes, bring a couple books on linguistics and teaching theory, to look the part of an English teacher. Prominently display them in your bookcase in your apartment. Also bring hiking and camping equipment. For some of the activities we will have you do, that equipment will be a good cover. And when you return to Langley, ask Joe to give you a copy of the Chinese driver's license exam in English. China doesn't recognize international driver's licenses, and you will definitely be renting cars, so study that test and take the test soon after you arrive in Urumqi.

We spent a couple more minutes talking and then he said it would be best if we left separately so he stayed there and I walked back to the entrance and caught a taxi back to the hotel.

I was sitting in the hotel bar that night drinking a beer, and more fully understanding the magnitude of what I was getting into. It was unsettling and honestly a bit exciting at the same time.

The following morning I caught a flight to Urumqi, the capital of Xinjiang. It took about four hours.

I thought Beijing was going to have the worst pollution I would see in China, but it was pristine compared to Urumqi. I walked out of the airport and the air pollution was atrocious. I was a bit concerned about the effects on my lungs and body in general that living here for months or years would have. I could think about that later as I had things to do.

I took a taxi from the airport to my hotel in downtown Urumqi. After I checked in, I called Ma Qi at Xinjiang Agricultural University. We agreed to meet the next morning at 10am.

I then called Li Zhen Zhen at Xinjiang Medical University. I would meet with her in two days at 11 am.

I left my hotel and walked around for a bit. I was expecting to see more Uyghurs than I did. I would say I saw three Han for every one Uyghur. I found a Uyghur restaurant nearby and went in. I could read some of the menu, which was in Uyghur, but remembering what Joe said, I did not let on that I could read it.

When the waiter came over, I pointed at some meat skewers and vegetables that people at the table next to me were eating, and asked for the same. The skewers had some strong spices on them. I couldn't identify all of them.

I finished eating and went back to the hotel. I was still feeling the jet lag and took a nap for a few hours.

For dinner, I wandered into a KFC near the hotel. I was curious to see the similarities and differences between this one and the ones in America.

The chicken and fries tasted the same, but I also noticed some local dishes on the menu.

The next morning I took a taxi to Xinjiang Agricultural University. I walked up to the main gate of the university and Ma Qi met me there.

She asked me questions like why I wanted to teach in China, why Xinjiang and if I had any teaching experience.

I asked her about the school, the job and the students. She couldn't tell me the breakdown of Han students to Uyghurs. The job would be teaching spoken English and writing up to twenty hours a week. She told me they had five foreign teachers. The salary would be approximately 3500 Renminbi (RMB) per month, or about five hundred U.S. Dollars. It was a typical salary for a teacher in this part of China, unless you were part of the teaching fellows program which would pay much more.

However, that included a free apartment, and flight allowance. Besides, salary was not an issue as Langley would cover what I needed, but while in China I would have to spend like my teaching salary was my only source of income.

We walked over to her office. She asked me to fill out an application. She also asked me to email her a couple letters of recommendation once I got back to America.

Before I left she walked me over to the building where the foreign teachers lived and showed me one of the apartments. It was a small one bedroom, but it was ok, and what I expected.

I left the university and walked around the area. I found a hole in the wall Chinese restaurant and went in.

I ordered a plate of Kung Pao Chicken and rice for 7 RMB, about a buck. It was very good. I finished and went back to the hotel and crashed.

I woke up in the evening, but was still feeling a bit lethargic and not hungry. I watched TV for a couple hours then went back to bed.

The next morning I met Li Zhen Zhen at the medical university and went through a very similar routine as the day before.

The following day I flew back to Beijing and spent one night there before flying back to DC.

I got back to the farm about 7 pm and found Joe. He asked me about the trip. I told him everything went well.

I told him Mike mentioned the Chinese driver's license exam, and that I would need to email letters of recommendation to the universities. He told me Michelle would handle that.

It was now the beginning of February 2007 and I was now undergoing various parts of tradecraft training. This consisted of everything from recruiting agents (even though I was led to believe I wouldn't be doing much of this), bypassing security measures, interrogating people and the basics of physical dead drops among other topics.

One day in March I went into Joe's office to remind him about the letters of recommendation. He was staring at his computer.

He yelled, "This is why we spent a trillion dollars in Iraq!"

I said, "What are you talking about?"

He said, "I'm reading an article about how Iraq will most likely award their first post-war oil contract to the Chinese."

I said, "So much for loyalty."

He said, "That's not all. Last month an agreement on price was reached for a gas pipeline from Iran to Pakistan and India. This is why we need to stay in

Afghanistan and keep drone bombing those fuckers in Pakistan."

I asked, "How does that prevent any of this?"

He replied, "It may not prevent China from buying Iraqi oil, but I guarantee you as long as we still have bases in Afghanistan and the violence continues there, China will not build an oil pipeline from Iran through Afghanistan to Xinjiang because of the risk of terrorist attacks on the pipeline. That means they have to put the oil on ships which costs them more money, and that's good for us. And as long as there is chaos and destabilization in Pakistan, China is not going make a deal with Iran and Pakistan to extend the gas pipeline to China, and that's also good for us. And I bet you we are able to talk India out of this deal."

We spoke a bit more and then I left. From my conversations with Joe and

Mike, it was clear what our priorities were in western China.

It was mostly about the resources and if that meant keeping a war going and destabilizing an entire region, so be it as long as it meant it was more difficult for China to exploit resources. Clearly human rights had nothing to do with our policy. The only time anything related to that was mentioned to me was in regards to not getting caught, so I was not tortured.

I knew at least some of the stuff Joe was saying was true. The drone bombings in Pakistan were incredibly unpopular and were destabilizing at least part of the country. They killed many innocent people, and everyone else in the region walked around with a certain fear that they might be next. We knew that bred more terrorism. Of course with our defense spending as high as it was, some might say we needed new and more enemies to justify that kind of spending. It is safe to say I felt conflicted, which is not a good attitude to have at the start of such a career.

A week later Michelle came and got me and we went to "my house" and checked my email. She pulled out two letters of recommendation, scanned them into the computer and I emailed them to both schools.

We left and she took me to a sporting goods store. We bought boots, a two man tent, and various other hiking and camping supplies.

In May I was contacted by the university in DC that handled the fellowship program. They invited me to DC two days later for an in person interview. They asked me to prepare a twenty minute lesson on any topic, which I would deliver to them.

I told Joe and Michelle. They were both happy. I was happy that I had taken the class on teacher training.

I prepared a lesson on compare and contrast writing. Joe asked me to deliver the lesson to he and Michelle, which surprised me, but I did so and it seemed to go ok. They even asked me a few questions about the topic to try to prepare me when I got questions on the day of the interview.

On the day of the interview, I left the farm at 6 am. Half way there, I noticed I picked up a tail, two actually. Really? They were still testing me on surveillance detection. I wrote down the make, model and license plates on the two vehicles as well as description of the occupants so I could report it to my superiors at the farm.

I arrived in DC and parked at the university. I found the department building and met some other teachers who were also waiting.

When they called me in, I delivered my lesson. They asked me some questions afterword about my lesson, and also asked me where I would like to go. I felt like telling them Iceland, but of course I said Xinjiang. We said our goodbyes and I went back to the farm.

Shortly after I got back, Joe came to my room and asked, "How'd it go?"

I replied, "It seemed fine. By the way, here's the info on the tails I picked up. Am I going to be tested on surveillance until I go to the airport to leave for China?"

He looked at me seriously and said, "Absolutely, because when you are in Urumqi, that hyperawareness might be the one thing that saves your life as well as the life of your asset, and don't you ever forget that."

Two weeks later the university notified me that I was accepted into the fellows program, and got my preferred choice of Xinjiang. I didn't know if it was my resume or the CIA asking the State Department to approve me, but regardless, I was accepted.

I told Joe and Michelle and they were both happy.

In late June, I received an information package from the university which contained information about China, information about health insurance and other housekeeping matters.

In August, I was to attend a four day orientation for new fellows. Before I left, Joe talked to me.

He told me, "Don't be too sociable at this pow wow. We've gone to great lengths to build a good cover for you, but I don't want some social butterfly chatting you up about Bangkok, and realizing you don't know what you're talking about."

I said, "Ok, I'll be a loner."

He said, "No, I don't want you to do that either. I want you somewhere in between the two, but try to avoid any conversations about Thailand, or God forbid if anyone has been to the same university we say you are from."

With that, I left for DC and checked into a hotel the night before it was to start.

The event was basically four days of reassuring us, and telling us what to expect. I found it a bit ironic considering the position required two years' experience teaching overseas, so everyone knew generally what to expect (except me).

One thing they did to comfort us was tell us if we had problems we could contact a Regional English language Officer (RELO) who worked out of the embassy.

I knew the last thing Langley wanted me doing was contacting the embassy, so I didn't plan on utilizing the RELO.

I got back to the farm, and was set to fly out the beginning of September. Before I left, Joe had a talk with me.

One thing he said was, "Normally, you are required to report any close and continuing contact with foreigners, including women. In your case, we don't want you to have close and continuing contact with any Han women. It will be too difficult for you to build credibility and rapport with the Uyghurs if you are known to be porking some Han woman or women."

One other very important tidbit he told me was that the CIA had a Han asset in Urumqi named Liu Bo.

He told me that the son of a high ranking Chinese Communist Party (CCP) official in Xinjiang came to the U.S. two years ago on a student visa to get a graduate degree.

He was met by agency personnel at the airport. Immigration pulled him into a room and there, two CIA officers told him we knew his TOEFL test-the test of English for foreigners, was faked and he would immediately be deported unless he helped us.

I asked, "What did he say?"

"He agreed," Joe replied.

It wasn't clear to me if the guy's test was really faked or they were just bullshitting the guy, and I didn't ask Joe.

Joe continued, "We told him if he would feed us information for five years, then he could go to school here, we would give him a green card and lots of cash. He's already given us some good information. He just finished graduate school and is now back in Xinjiang. You are going to meet him every other Saturday morning, starting two weeks from tomorrow, unless you detect surveillance, in which case you pop into some random restaurant and eat your nice Chinese breakfast. Then you go back to your university. Assuming no surveillance, you will meet him at Nanhu Lake at 8 am."

I interjected, "I'm assuming I'm never to bring my cellphone with me to the meets?"

"Absolutely, no cellphones or any other electronics. Also, don't exchange phone numbers or email addresses with Bo. When you two are together, if you are seen by people who know him or you, your story is just that you are friends. If they ask how you know each other, you met in a restaurant, and leave it at that. Bo has been told the same thing. Now, Bo may have information for you or he may not. When you meet him in two weeks, try to find out about upcoming strike hard campaigns. That's what they call their attacks on Uyghurs. We have signals intelligence that they may be planning a new one. Ask him about it. Also, ask him about any leadership changes in the party in Xinjiang and what new plans they have for oil and gas exploration there as well as deals with other countries. Then when you meet Mike you will give the information to him, and he will give you money to give to Bo."

"When will my first meet with Mike be?" I asked.

He said, "National holiday. On October first, you will fly to Chengdu. On October second, you will meet Mike at the Peter Pan Italian Restaurant at 11 am. Again, don't bring any phones or other electronics. Give him whatever information you've gotten so far from Bo. At that time, he'll arrange your next meet."

Joe then said, "Lastly, on the weekends you are not meeting with Bo, we have a Uyghur asset you will be meeting on Sunday mornings. His name is Ziya. You will meet with him every other Sunday morning at 8 am at People's Park. The same rules about electronics apply. He is wired in with the Uyghur community in Urumqi as well as Kashgar. When we want groups to take some action, you tell Ziya, and he will make it happen. You will also be funneling money to him. Mike will get into the details of your interactions with Ziya more when you see him in October."

I had a week to go to California and visit family and tie up loose ends. Then I flew back to DC, and spent two nights at the farm. Joe then drove me to the airport in DC and I flew direct to Beijing, and on to Xinjiang.